Daisy Box

3½"x3½"x6¼" clear
* acrylic box*
7/16" white ball & stick
* letter stickers*
1⅓ yards of ⅝" wide white
* dots on pink grosgrain*
* ribbon*
30" of 6" wide pink tulle
¾" wide daisy button
dimensional paints: white,
* pink*
22-gauge wire
wire cutters
basic supplies (see inside
* the front cover)*

1 Cut a 15" length of ribbon and glue it around the lid side, ¼" from the bottom edge. Paint five wavy white lines evenly spaced, ½" apart on each side of the box; let dry. Paint four pink dots evenly spaced between each row, staggering the rows as shown.

2 With the tulle, make a puffy bow (see inside the back cover) with six 2" loops. Glue the bow to the lid top center. With the remaining ribbon, make a puffy bow with eight 1½" loops. Glue the bow to the tulle bow center. Cut the shank from the button, then glue the button to the pink bow center. Use the letter stickers to personalize the box.

Flower Pot

5½"x5½" white ceramic
* flower pot*
19" of ⅝" wide white dots on
* yellow grosgrain ribbon*
six ¾" wide daisy buttons
pink enamel paint
yellow medium point paint pen
yellow dimensional paint

enamel surface cleaner and
* conditioner*
enamel clear gloss glaze
½" wide flat paintbrush
basic supplies (see inside the front
* cover)*

1 Follow the manufacturer's directions to clean the pot surface. Paint ½" wide pink stripes, ¾" apart around the pot as shown; let dry. Follow the manufacturer's directions to apply glaze to the surface; let dry.

2 Use the dimensional paint to make a wavy line along the center of each pink stripe; let dry. With the paint pen, write your name between each stripe; let dry. Glue the ribbon around the pot rim. Cut the shanks from the buttons, then glue the buttons evenly spaced onto the ribbon.

Piggy Bank

2¾"x3" white ceramic piggy
* bank*
7/16" pink ball & stick letter
* stickers*
9" of ⅛" wide white dots on pink
* satin ribbon*

dimensional paints: white, yellow
paint pens: pink fine point, black
* medium point*
basic supplies (see inside the
* front cover)*

1 Paint ⅜" wide pink half circles for each inner ear; let dry. With the ribbon, make a shoestring bow (see inside the back cover) with ⅜" loops and ½" tails. Glue the bow below the snout.

2 Use the tip of the white paint bottle to draw a row three flowers on the right side, each with five petals; let dry. Paint yellow dots in each flower center and add black eyes and snout details; let dry. Use the letter stickers to personalize the bank below the flowers.

1

Trinket Box

2¼"x2¼"x4" clear acrylic box
⁷⁄₁₆" navy blue ball & stick letter stickers
10" of 1¼" wide purple/pink/aqua trim with flowers
10" of 1½" wide yellow/orange/aqua/purple/lime green beaded fringe with ⅜" wide white satin band
rhinestones: one 15mm purple, four 5mm clear
paint pens: purple, dark blue
basic supplies (see inside the front cover)

1 Paint ¼" wide purple squares ¼" apart along the bottom edges of the box sides. Paint a blue dot on each square.

2 Glue the satin band along the bottom edge of the lid. Glue the trim around the sides of the lid, covering the satin band. Glue the purple rhinestone to the lid top center and a clear rhinestone in each corner. Use the letter stickers to personalize the box.

Pencil Box

2½"x1¾"x7½" clear plastic box with dividers
⁷⁄₁₆" navy blue ball & stick letter stickers
9½" of 1¼" wide purple/pink/aqua trim with flowers
fourteen 3mm dark blue rhinestones
paint pens: purple, dark blue
basic supplies (see inside the front cover)

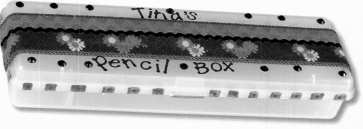

1 Paint ⅜" wide purple squares along the lid sides. Paint a blue dot on each square. Glue the trim across the lid, wrapping the ends to the inside.

2 Use the letter stickers to personalize the box. Glue the rhinestones to the lid as shown.

Crayon Tin

6¾"x5½" round white metal pail with handle
¾" black letter stickers
1¼ yards of ⅝" wide crayons on white satin ribbon
2 yards of 1½" wide white dots on red satin ribbon with wire edges
black medium point paint pen
crayons: 1 blue, 1 yellow
basic supplies (see inside the front cover)

1 Paint black dots around the edge of the lid. Cut a 22" length from each ribbon and glue them along the box bottom, overlapping as shown. Use the remaining red ribbon to make a puffy bow (see inside the back cover) with eight 2½" loops and 5" tails. Glue the bow to the lid top center. Wrap a tail to the inside on each side and glue to secure.

2 Use the remaining crayon ribbon to make a puffy bow with a center loop, eight 2" loops and no tails. Glue the bow to the dots bow center. Glue the crayons to the bow center loop. Use the letter stickers to personalize the tin.

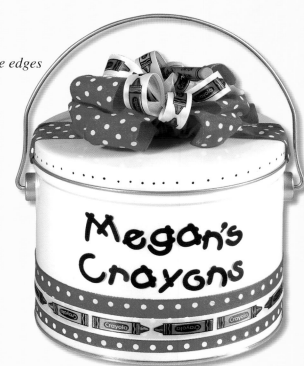

Candy Holder

1⅛"x1⅛"x2¾" clear acrylic box
⁷⁄₁₆" black ball & stick letter stickers
1" wide black/white gingham ribbon flower with green satin
  ribbon leaves
12" of ⅝" wide black/white gingham ribbon
medium point black paint pen
red candies
basic supplies (see inside the front cover)

1 Fill the box with candies and replace the lid. Draw four black dots on each side of the box bottom and lid sides.

2 Wrap the ribbon around the box bottom, pull the ends even above the lid and knot to secure. Trim the tails to 1", then cut an inverted "V" into each end. Glue the ribbon flower centered on the knot. Use the letter stickers to personalize the box front as shown.

> **LeNae's Suggestion:** *This mini candy box works great as a party favor. Make one for each guest and fill them with small candies. Choose various color ribbons and top it off with fun plastic ornaments!*

Hat Box

6¼"x5¾"x4" white metal suitcase with a 1½" tall black
  plastic handle
⁷⁄₁₆" black ball & stick letter stickers
three ⅝" wide ladybug buttons
20" of 1½" wide white dots on black ribbon with wire edges
  12" of 1½" wide red grosgrain ribbon
    22-gauge wire
      wire cutters
        basic supplies (see inside the front cover)

1 Cut a 6½" length of the dots ribbon. Fold each end under ¼", then glue it centered on the suitcase front as shown. With the red ribbon, make a loopy bow (see inside the front cover) with two 2½" loops. Glue the bow to the top edge of the dotted ribbon.

2 With the remaining dots ribbon, make a shoestring bow with 2" loops and 2" tails. Trim the tails at an angle, then glue the dots bow centered on the red bow. Use the wire cutters to cut the shanks from each button. Glue one button to the bow center and the two remaining buttons evenly spaced on the ribbon strip. Use the letter stickers to personalize the suitcase front.

Flower Power Boxes

clear acrylic boxes:
one 2¼"x2¼"x4",
one 1⅛"x1⅛"x2¾"
ribbons: 24" of ⅞" wide bright pink
satin with white daisies and green
trim, 6" of ¼" wide white picot
satin ribbon
white craft foam flowers: two 2⅜",
one 1¼" wide

lime green craft foam circles: two
¾", one ⅜" wide
fine tip paint pens: lime green, pink,
dark pink
basic supplies (see inside the front
cover)

1 For the large box: Glue pink ribbon around the sides of the lid. Glue a large flower to two sides on top of the ribbon. Glue a large green circle to each flower center. Draw dark pink dots on the petals of each flower. Draw staggered rows of green dots along the lid and top and bottom edges of the box. Write your name with the pink pen, then draw green dots on each letter as shown.

2 For the small box: Cut the remaining pink ribbon in half. Fold each end under ¼" and glue one length to the lid edge, down the box side, along the bottom and up the opposite side. Repeat for the other ribbon length. Glue the picot ribbon to the lid sides. Glue the small circle to the small flower center, then glue the flower to the lid top center. Draw dark pink dots on the petals.

Rhinestone Tin

6¾"x5½" white metal pail with handle
blue moons and white stars washable art glaze
light blue rhinestones: four 25mm hearts, one 15mm
round, three 8mm round, seven 6mm round, 3mm
round (enough to spell your initials)
clear rhinestones: four 25mm hearts, sixteen 6mm
round

½ yard of three different textures of dark blue and
aqua fibers
spray sealer
liquid varnish
½" wide flat paintbrush
basic supplies (see inside the front cover)

1 Remove the lid. Lightly spray the lid and pail with sealer; let dry. Follow the manufacturer's directions to apply the art glaze on the lid; let dry. Apply varnish onto the glaze; let dry.

2 Glue the 15mm rhinestone to the lid top center. Glue three 8mm and three 6mm clear rhinestones evenly spaced around the center stone.

3 Glue two blue and two clear hearts evenly spaced along the top edge of the pail front as shown. Repeat for the back. Glue a 6mm blue stone between each heart. Glue the remaining clear round rhinestones along the bottom. Use the 3mm stones to spell your initials; let dry. Cut two 9" lengths of each of three fibers. Hold one of each length together and tie them around the handle base. Repeat for the other handle base.

Floral Tins

3"x4" white metal rectangle tin
2"x3" white metal oval tin
spring floral pick with
  one 2" lavender daisy,
  five 1½" purple pansies,
  two 3" lavender sprigs,
  four ¾" dark pink daisies,
  three ½" pink wild flowers,
  three 1"-1½" green ivy leaves and
  six 1½"x2" green rose leaves

light green round tags:
  1⅜", 1" wide
33" of 1⅜" wide white/pink/
  green plaid satin ribbon
  with wire edges
four 18" strands of raffia
black fine point pen
basic supplies (see inside
  the front cover)

1 Cut the ribbon into 18" and 15" lengths. Place two raffia strands centered on the 18" ribbon and wrap them around the rectangle tin sides; knot to secure. Repeat for the remaining ribbon and raffia on the oval tin. Cut an inverted "V" into each tail. From the floral pick, cut the large daisy, two pansies, two small daisies, two small wild flowers, three rose leaves, two ivy leaves and one lavender sprig. Set the remaining flowers and leaves aside for step 3.

2 For the rectangle tin lid: Glue the rose leaves onto the lid so they fan out from the center. Glue the ivy leaves, extending outward, to fill empty spaces. Glue the large daisy to the center, then the pansies behind the daisy. Glue the lavender sprig extending outward from under the upper left of the daisy, then glue a wild flower to each side of the daisy. Glue the small daisies clustered to the lower right of the large daisy.

3 For the oval tin lid: Glue three rose leaves and the ivy leaf so they fan out from the center. Glue the three pansies clusters in the center. Glue one wild flower and the lavender sprig extending outward to the left and one wild flower extending outward from the lower right of the pansies. Glue the daisies clustered between the pansies and lower right wild flower.

4 Use the pen to personalize the tags. Glue each tag hanger underneath the flowers as shown, to hang down onto the box side.

LeNae's Suggestion: *These tins make great favors and can be made very inexpensively for large groups. One floral pick covers two lids and the tags come in packages of 8-10. What a lovely idea!*

Camping Gear Case

6$\frac{1}{2}$"x3$\frac{1}{2}$"x9" plastic box with 2$\frac{1}{2}$"
  handle
$\frac{3}{4}$" black letter stickers
camping rub-on transfers
black medium point paint pen
basic supplies (see inside the front cover)

1 Draw a dash-dot border along the bottom edge of the box. Repeat for a border below the lid.

2 Follow the manufacturer's directions to apply the transfers onto the box as shown. Use the letter stickers to spell out "Camp Out Gear" on the lid. Add a name to the center front.

LeNae's Suggestion:
These boxes make great travel containers for children. Fill them full of their favorite toys or snacks!

Fire Chief Case

5"x5$\frac{1}{2}$"x9$\frac{1}{2}$" clear plastic box
  with red trim and 1$\frac{1}{2}$" handle
$\frac{7}{16}$" red ball & stick letter
  stickers
fire truck rub-on transfers
black paint for plastics

black medium point paint pen
1" square compressed sponge
paper plate
basic supplies (see inside the
  front cover)

1 Pour a quarter size puddle of paint onto the paper plate. Moisten the sponge, dip it into the paint, then press it onto the bottom of the lid to form a row of squares 1" apart. Repeat for another row on top, staggering the squares to form a checkerboard. Repeat for five rows on the lid; let dry.

2 Follow the manufacturer's directions to apply the fire trucks to the box as shown. Use the letter stickers to personalize the box. Draw a dash-dot border below the lid as shown.

Basketball Card Tin

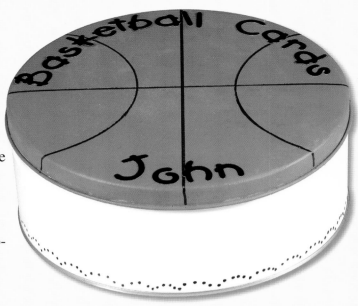

8"x3" white round tin
¾" black letter stickers
terra cotta acrylic paint
matte finish liquid sealer
black medium point pain pen

1" wide foam brush
5" wide cardboard circle
paper plate
basic supplies (see inside the front cover)

1 Remove the lid. Apply a thin layer of sealer to the lid with the foam brush; let dry. Pour a quarter size puddle of paint onto the paper plate. Dip the brush into the paint, press it onto the lid, then lift straight up for texture. Continue until the lid is covered and let dry.

2 Draw a straight line from top-to-bottom, then side-to-side on the lid. Place half of the circle onto one side of the lid and trace around it. Repeat for the other side.

3 Draw a scallop dots border along the tin bottom edge. Use the letter stickers to spell out "Basketball Cards" on the lid top as shown, then add a name to the bottom.

Basketball Frame

7" square white ceramic frame with 3"x4½" opening
⁷⁄₁₆" ball & stick letter and number stickers: red, black
sports rub-on transfers
basic supplies (see inside the front cover)

1 Use the black stickers to personalize the frame top with your name and the year at the frame bottom. Place the same red sticker slightly off center of each black sticker for a shadow effect.

2 Cut out two basketballs, slamdunk, star border and four single stars from the rub-ons. Follow the manufacturer's directions to apply them to the frame as shown.

Basketball Box

2¼"x2¼"x4" clear acrylic box
⁷⁄₁₆" ball & stick letter stickers: red, black
sports rub-on transfers
yellow medium point paint pen
basic supplies (see inside the front cover)

1 Use the black letter stickers to personalize the frame top with your name and the year at the frame bottom. Place the same red letter sticker slightly off center of each letter for a shadow effect. Draw a dot border along the top and bottom edges of the lid and the box bottom as shown.

2 Cut six stars, one basketball and one basketball in a square from the rub-ons. Follow the manufacturer's directions to apply the transfers to the box as shown.

Daisy Pot

5½"x5½" white ceramic
    flower pot
7/16" black letter stickers
daisy rub-on transfers
enamel glass paints: yellow,
    light blue
enamel surface cleaner and
    conditioner

enamel gloss glaze
natural sea sponge
1" wide foam brush
paper plate
basic supplies (see inside
    the front cover)

1 Follow the manufacturer's directions to apply the cleaner to the pot surface. Pour a quarter size puddle of yellow paint onto the paper plate. Moisten the sponge, dip it into the paint and press it onto the pot rim. Repeat to cover the rim and let dry. Rinse the sponge and pour blue paint onto the plate. Lightly sponge the pot sides blue and let dry. Follow the manufacturer's directions to apply glaze to the painted surfaces and let dry.

2 Cut the daisy border strips into ten 3-square pieces and cut out five large daisies from the rub-ons. Apply the daisies evenly spaced around the rim, then apply two rows of squares between each daisy. Follow the manufacturer's directions to apply glaze over the transfers; let dry. Use the letter stickers to personalize the pot.

Bath Pail

6¾"x5½" round white metal pail with handle
12"x12" Paper Pizazz™ Bright Tints Pink Swirls patterned
    paper
7/16" black letter stickers
1¼ yards of 1½" wide purple sheer ribbon with wire edges
9" of purple fiber
25mm purple heart rhinestone
paint pens: fine point dark pink, medium point purple

1⅝"x3¼" white tag
bath accessories: foot brush, plastic green
    frog bath toy, 4-colored bath scrunchy,
    bottles of bath bubbles or gel
excelsior (enough to fill the tin)
basic supplies (see inside the front cover)

1 Remove the lid. Cut the swirls paper into two 3"x12" strips. Glue the strips to form a band around the tin, ¼" from the bottom edge. Wrap the ribbon around the swirls band, knot twice at the front and cut an inverted "V" into each tail.

2 Draw purple dots ¼" apart along the bottom edge of the tin. Repeat for another row around the top, just below the ridge. Draw a row of pink dots above the ridge, near the top.

3 Cut a 1⅝"x1⅛" piece of swirls paper and glue it near the bottom edge of the tag. Glue the rhinestone onto the swirls. Use the letter stickers to personalize the tag. Use the fiber to tie the tag to the handle base. Insert excelsior into the tin, then arrange the bath accessories on top.

Easter Basket Pail

6¾"x7¼" round white metal pail with handle
painted "spring-theme" wood pieces: six 1"
    pink tulips, six 1" yellow daffodils, one 1¼"
    tan bunny, one 1½" butterfly
1 yard of ⅝" wide pink sheer ribbon
acrylic paints for metal: light blue, orange,
    yellow, teal
medium point paint pens: yellow, pink, navy
    blue, purple, green, yellow
two 2½"x4" rectangles of compressed
    sponge
spray matte sealer
tracing paper
Easter grass and pastel plastic eggs
paper plate
basic supplies (see inside the front cover)

1 Remove the lid. Trace the egg
pattern and place it over the
sponge. Cut out four egg shapes.
Pour a quarter size puddle of each
paint onto the paper plate. Using
both sides of the sponges randomly
sponge the eggs along the bottom
edge of the pail at different angles
and let dry.

2 Use the paint pens to decorate
the eggs with stripes, dots and
zig zags as shown. Draw clusters of
4-5 blades of grass with the green pen
along the pail bottom edge. Draw ¼"
dashes along the pail top on the ridge.

3 Write "Happy Easter" and your
name on the front with the blue
paint pen. Draw yellow dots around
each letter, then draw ⅝" yellow squares
¾" apart along the top rim. Lightly
spray the pail with sealer and let dry.

4 Glue the wood pieces to the pail as shown. Cut the ribbon
in half. Wrap one length around a handle base and tie it
into a shoestring bow (see inside the back cover) with 1½"
loops and 6" tails. Trim the tails at an angle. Repeat for a bow
on the opposite handle base. Insert the grass into the tin, then
place the eggs on top.

LeNae's Suggestion: *With a few simple changes,
create an adorable pail for a boy. Choose animal
or sports wood pieces to decorate the bottom edge.
These durable pails will last for years!*

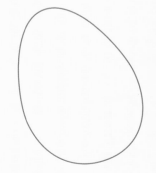

Stars & Stripes Box

8"x3" round white tin
12"x12" Paper Pizazz™ navy with stars patterned paper
¾" red letter stickers
stars & stripes rub-on transfers
decoupage glue
1" wide foam brush
basic supplies (see inside the front cover)

1 Remove the lid. Tear the straight edges from the patterned paper into 1"-2" squares, keeping the straight edge intact. Apply decoupage glue to the back side of a piece, then place the straight edge along the lid side edge, wrapping the torn edges to the lid top. Repeat to cover the lid sides, overlapping the pieces. Tear more paper pieces into various shapes. Apply glue to the back sides and place them overlapping on the top. Apply a coat of decoupage glue along the covered lid surface and let dry.

2 Cut the stars and stripes rub-on border into eight 2" lengths. Follow the manufacturer's instructions to place the pieces evenly spaced around the tin sides. Cut eight pairs of small stars and place them centered between the stripes. Cut out eight large stars and place them evenly spaced along the lid top edge. Use the letter stickers to spell "USA" in the lid center and your name along the top and bottom as shown.

Watermelon Box

7"x2¾" round red tin
⁷⁄₁₆" black ball & stick letter stickers
24" of ¾" wide red/white gingham ribbon
acrylic paints: white, lime green, medium green
black dimensional paint
liquid matte sealer
3" wide round sponge
paper plate
toothpick
basic supplies (see inside the front cover)

1 Remove the lid. Use the sponge to apply sealer to the lid and tin; let dry. Rinse the sponge. Pour a quarter size puddle of medium green paint onto the paper plate, press the sponge in the paint and then along the box sides. Repeat to sponge the lid, leaving a 5" wide round circle in the lid center; let dry.

2 Replace the lid. Rinse the sponge. Pour a quarter size puddle of lime green paint onto the paper plate. Sponge 1" wide stripes extending from the tin bottom edge up onto the lid, each 2" apart; let dry. Rinse the sponge and apply sealer over the painted surface; let dry.

3 For the seeds: squeeze black paint in teardrop dots along the outer edge of the red circle; let dry. Dip the toothpick into the

white paint and press it onto each black dot. Wrap the ribbon around the box, below the lid, fold the overlapping ends under and glue to secure. Use the letter stickers on the lid to personalize the tin.

Craft Tin

7"x2¾" round red tin
7/16" black letter stickers
1⅔ yards of ⅝" wide white gimp braid
18"x22" red/white gingham cotton dish towel
1¼" wide white 2-hole button
red embroidery floss
two 8" squares of polyester fiberfill
sewing needle
drill with ⅛" bit
basic supplies (see inside the front cover)

1 Remove the lid. Place the towel flat, place the lid on top and cut the towel 1" larger than the lid; set the circle aside. Drill two holes 1/16" apart into the lid center. Stack the fiberfill on the lid, trimming the excess. Place the towel circle centered on the lid top and glue the edges around the lid sides, slightly pleating along the edge.

2 Thread the needle with floss. Place the button centered on the gingham, insert the needle into the button hole and through the drill hole and up through the other drill hole and button hole. Pull the thread ends even and knot twice to secure. Trim the floss ends to ½".

3 Cut two 48" lengths of braid. Glue one length around the lid sides and the other around the tin bottom. Use the letter stickers to spell "Create ❧ Wish ★ Craft ❧ Dream ★ Look ❧ Joy ★ Play" along the bottom sides.

Daisy Sewing Tin

8"x3" round white tin
7/16" black ball & stick letter stickers
two 8½"x11" rectangles of bright pink felt
2½" wide foam ball
5" square of yellow/white gingham fabric
¾ yard of 1⅜" wide yellow/white gingham ribbon
white embroidery floss
serrated knife
sewing needle
straight pins
tracing paper
basic supplies (see inside the front cover)

1 Wrap the ribbon around the tin center, fold the end under and glue to secure. Use the letter stickers on the ribbon to personalize the tin.

2 Trace the petal pattern onto tracing paper and cut it out. Pin the pattern to the felt and cut around it. Repeat for 10 more petals. Thread the needle with three strands of floss and sew a running stitch (see inside the back cover) around each petal edge. Place a petal on the lid, then place another petal overlapping on its left. Repeat with the remaining petals, leaving the lid center exposed, then glue in place.

3 Cut the foam ball in half; set aside one piece for another project. Cover one piece with the gingham, gluing the edges under. Glue the half ball to the lid center. Insert straight pins into the center.

11

Tux Bear Bank

shirt

inner ear

collar

9½" tall white ceramic bear bank
enamel glass paints: black, red, pink
paint pens: fine point black, medium point pink,
  metallic silver
white dimensional paint
enamel cleaner and conditioner
enamel clear gloss glaze
½" wide flat paintbrush
tracing paper
basic supplies (see inside the front cover)

1 Follow the manufacturer's directions to clean the ceramic surface. Trace the patterns and cut them out. Place the shirt front piece below the bow and use the black pen to trace the bottom point. Measure ¾" from his hand bottom edge and mark a straight line across the hand top for the sleeve bottom edge. Repeat for the other hand.

2 Paint the bow red; let dry. Paint the inner ears pink; let dry. Paint the surface below the bear's head black, excluding the bow tie, "V-neck" and hands. Paint the nose and eyes black; let dry. Paint a second coat of black and let dry. Use your fingertip to apply pink paint to each cheek and let dry.

3 With the black paint pen, draw the mouth inside the indents on the face as shown. Make the bow highlights and four dots for buttons on the shirt front. Draw a line ¼" below each sleeve, then draw a dot centered below each sleeve.

4 Hold the collar pattern to the right of the bow and trace around the outer edge with the silver pen. Turn the pattern over and repeat for a left side collar. Draw a silver dot below the right collar bottom point. Draw a straight 1" line from the shirt, then a line across the tummy to each hand, continuing the line on the other side of each hand to meet in the back. To outline the shoes, draw a line ½" above the bottom edge in the back and 1" in the front, encircling the bear. Draw a pant's line in the front and back to outline the legs. Let dry.

5 Follow the manufacturer's directions to apply glaze over the entire surface; let dry. Add a dot of white dimensional paint on each cheek; let dry. Use the silver pen to personalize the bear near his right ear.

Ballerina Bear Bank

9½" tall white ceramic bear bank
¾ yards of ⅝" wide pink
    grosgrain ribbon
1¼" yards of 6" wide pink tulle
⅜" wide satin ribbon roses with
    green ribbon leaves: 8 pink,
    7 white
pink enamel glass paint

dark pink paint pen
white dimensional paint
white thread
sewing needle
liquid matte sealer
½" wide flat paintbrush
basic supplies (see inside the
    front cover)

1 Use the paint pen to draw a straight line ¾" above the bottom edge around the bear's feet and color the area below pink. Draw a second line 1½" above the first line, an "X" between the lines on each foot, then a small bow on top as shown. Draw ⅝" wide pink half circles for each inner ear; let dry.

2 Use the paintbrush to apply a light coat of sealer to the bear's tummy, back, cheeks and to the left of the right ear; let dry. Cut 8" from the tulle and set aside for step 4. Cut the remaining tulle into two 18" lengths. Fold each piece in half lengthwise and use the needle and thread to gather the folded edge on one to 6" and the other to 7". Glue the 6" piece to the tummy and the 7" to the back to form the tutu.

3 Glue three white and three pink roses evenly spaced on the gathered portion of the skirt front, alternating colors. Repeat for the back with four white and three pink roses. Cut 2½" from the ribbon and set aside. Wrap the remaining ribbon around the bear's neck and tie it in the front into a shoestring bow (see inside the front cover) with 1½" loops and tails. Cut an inverted "V" into each tail. Glue a pink rose to the bow center.

4 Use your fingertip to apply pink paint to each cheek and let dry. Add a dot of white dimensional paint on each cheek. Cut the remaining tulle into two 3"x4" rectangles. Place the pieces together, then use the needle and thread to sew the center together to form a bow. Cut an inverted "V" into the ends of the remaining ribbon, then sew it centered on the tulle bow front. Glue a pink rose to the bow center, then glue the bow to the left of her right ear. Use the pink pen to personalize the bear as shown.

Ballerina Box

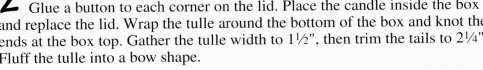

2¼"x2¼"x3" clear acrylic box
12"x12" Paper Pizazz™ Soft Tints
    pink/yellow gingham patterned
    paper
Paper Pizazz™ Janie Dawson's
    Girlfriends Stickers

7/16" white ball & stick letter
    stickers
18" of 6" wide light pink tulle
four ½" wide pink buttons
2"x2¾" candle
basic supplies (see inside the
    front cover)

1 Cut a 1¾"x9½" strip of gingham paper, wrap it around the center of the box and glue the overlapping ends in the back to secure. Apply a ballerina sticker to the strip on the box front. Use the letter stickers to personalize the box as shown.

2 Cut a 1¾" square of gingham paper and glue it centered on the top lid. Glue a button to each corner on the lid. Place the candle inside the box and replace the lid. Wrap the tulle around the bottom of the box and knot the ends at the box top. Gather the tulle width to 1½", then trim the tails to 2¼". Fluff the tulle into a bow shape.

Photo Frame

7" square white ceramic frame with a 3"x4½" opening
12"x12" Paper Pizazz™ Soft Tints yellow gingham
 patterned paper
7/16" white ball & stick letter stickers
four ¼" wide yellow buttons
28" of 3/16" wide white/yellow satin ribbon
yellow dimensional paint
metallic gold pen
solid white paper
basic supplies (see inside the front cover)

1 Cut a 1½"x5¼" rectangle of gingham paper. Glue it to the white paper, with an ⅛" edge. Glue the matted gingham centered onto the right side of the frame. Draw gold dashes along the gingham edges. Glue a button to each corner. Use the letter stickers to personalize the frame as shown.

2 Cut the ribbon into four 7" lengths. With each length, make a shoestring bow (see inside the front cover) with ⅜" loops and tails. glue a bow to each corner of the frame opening. Squeeze small yellow dots along the opening edge as shown. Insert a photo into the frame.

Yellow Collage Suitcase

4"x7"x5⅛" white metal suitcase with a 2⅜" tall
 black plastic handle
12"x12" Paper Pizazz™ Soft Tints patterned papers:
 yellow gingham, yellow stripes, yellow dots
7/16" black ball & stick letter stickers
26" of 3/16" wide white/yellow satin ribbon
18" of ⅛" wide white satin ribbon

3/8" wide white satin ribbon rose with green ribbon
 leaves
white acrylic paint
1" wide foam brush
decoupage glue
basic supplies (see inside the front cover)

1 Paint the metal edges of the lid and box white; let dry. Apply a second coat; let dry. Tear 1" along the straight edges of each paper. Apply decoupage glue to the back of a piece, then place the straight edge even with the lid top edge. Repeat, alternating patterns in an overlapping pattern along the lid, rounding the corner pieces. Repeat to cover the box bottom. Randomly tear more pieces from the patterned papers to cover the remaining surface of the lid and box. Apply a coat of sealer to the papered surfaces and let dry.

2 Cut a 8" length from the white/yellow ribbon. Hold the 18" ribbon lengths together and make a loopy bow (see inside the front cover) with four 1½" loops and two 2½" tails, using the 8" length to tie the bow at the center. Knot each tail. Glue the

bow to the suitcase clasp, allowing the clasp to open and close freely. Glue the rose to the bow center. Use the letter stickers to personalize the suitcase.

Pink & Yellow Collage Suitcase

6¼"x5¾"x4" metal suitcase with a 1½" tall black plastic handle
12"x12" Paper Pizazz™ Soft Tints patterned papers: yellow/pink
  gingham, pink swirls, yellow dots
7/16" black ball & stick letter stickers
28" of 3/16" wide white/yellow satin ribbon
20" of 1/8" wide white dots on pink satin ribbon
3/8" wide pink satin ribbon rose with green ribbon leaves
1" wide foam brush
decoupage glue
basic supplies (see inside the front cover)

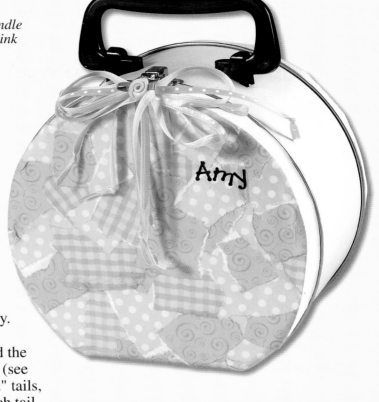

1 Randomly tear 1"-1½" pieces from each patterned paper, trimming one side in a curve to match the lid outer edge. Apply decoupage glue to the back of a piece, then place the curved edge even with the lid top edge. Repeat, alternating patterns in an overlapping pattern along the lid. Repeat to cover the suitcase back. Randomly tear more pieces from the patterned papers to cover the remaining surface of the lid and back. Apply a coat of sealer to the papered surfaces and let dry.

2 Cut a 8" length from the white/yellow ribbon. Hold the 20" ribbon lengths together and make a loopy bow (see inside the front cover) with four 1½" loops and two 2½" tails, using the 8" length to tie the bow at the center. Knot each tail. Glue the bow to the suitcase clasp, allowing the clasp to open and close freely. Glue the rose to the bow center. Use the letter stickers to personalize the suitcase.

1 Cut a 5½"x8½" rectangle of dots paper. Glue it centered on the lid, wrapping the back over the hinge and under the front. Cut a 3½"x5" rectangle of yellow gingham. Glue it to the white paper, with an 1/8" edge. Glue the matted gingham paper centered on the lid.

Supply Box

8½"x5"x2¼" white posterboard box with hinged lid
12"x12" Paper Pizazz™ Soft Tints patterned papers:
  yellow gingham, yellow dots
7/16" white ball & stick letter stickers
four ¼" wide yellow buttons
1 yard of 3/16" wide white/yellow satin ribbon
metallic gold pen
solid white paper
basic supplies (see inside the front cover)

2 Draw gold dashes along the gingham edges. Glue a button to each corner. Use the letter stickers to personalize the gingham as shown. Cut the ribbon into four 9" lengths. Glue one length end ¼" onto the box bottom front, 5/8" from the side, so it wraps to the front and top. Repeat for the other side. Glue another length end ¼" onto the bottom back, 5/8" from the side, so it wraps to the back and top. Repeat for the other side. Hold the left side ribbons together and tie into a shoestring bow with 1" loops and tails. Repeat for the right side pair of ribbons.

Heart Box

5¼"x5"x2¾" white ceramic heart box
⁷⁄₁₆" black letter and number stickers
18" of 1¼" wide dark pink/clear beaded fringe
  with ⅜" wide dark pink satin band
ten 8mm clear rhinestones
pink hearts washable art glaze
liquid matte varnish
½" wide flat paintbrush
basic supplies (see inside the front cover)

1 Remove the lid. Follow the manufacturer's directions to apply the hearts glaze to the lid and box sides; let dry. Apply varnish over the glazed surfaces and let dry.

2 Glue the rhinestones evenly spaced around the lid as shown. Use the stickers to personalize the lid. Glue the satin band of the beaded fringe along the top edge of the box. Place the lid on the box.

Rhinestone Box

2⅝"x1¾" white round ceramic box
light blue enamel glass paint
white fine point paint pen
round rhinestones: 24 clear 3mm,
  11 light blue 3mm, four clear 10mm,
  6 pink 15mm, 2 light blue 15mm,
  3 clear 15mm
pink square 25mm rhinestone
enamel cleaner and conditioner
enamel clear gloss glaze
½" wide flat paintbrush
basic supplies (see inside the front cover)

1 Follow the manufacturer's directions to clean the ceramic surface. Remove the lid. Paint the lid and box light blue; let dry. Apply a second coat of paint; let dry. Apply a coat of glaze over the painted areas and let dry.

2 For the lid: Glue the square rhinestone centered on the top. Glue a 15mm pink rhinestone at each corner of the square. Glue a 10mm clear rhinestone between each pair of pink rhinestones. Glue a 3mm clear rhinestone next to each 10mm clear stone, then glue a 3mm blue stone on each side of the 3mm clear stone. Glue sixteen 3mm clear rhinestones evenly spaced around the lid sides.

3 For the box: Glue a 15mm clear rhinestone to the front, left and right side. Glue a 15mm pink stone between the front and left clear stone and one to the back. Glue a 15mm blue between the front and right clear stones and one between the left clear and back pink stone. Glue the remaining 3mm stones between the large ones. Write your name in white along the top and bottom edges as a border.

Blue Beaded Heart Box

3"x1¾" white ceramic heart box
¼ cup of micro mosaic blue glass bead mix
* with various seed, bugle and micro marbles*
rhinestones: one 14mm clear teardrop,
* three 3mm light blue*
black fine tip paint pen
Terrifically Tacky Tape™
liquid matte varnish
½" wide flat paintbrush
basic supplies (see inside the front cover)

1 Cover the lid top with the tape, trimming around the heart shape. Remove the tape backing and sprinkle the bead mix onto the tape, using your fingers to press the beads in place.

2 Use the paintbrush to apply a coat of varnish over the beads and let dry. Glue the teardrop rhinestone to the center of the lid. Use the pen to write "Love You Mom" along the box sides. Glue a blue rhinestone between the words "Mom" and "Love".

Tutti Frutti Beaded Box

2¼"x2¼"x4" clear acrylic box
⁷⁄₁₆" white ball & stick letter stickers
¼ cup of micro mosaic tutti frutti glass bead mix
* with various seed, bugle and micro marbles*
liquid matte varnish
Terrifically Tacky Tape™
½" wide flat paintbrush
tracing paper
basic supplies (see inside the front cover)

1 Cut three 2½" lengths of tape. Place one length along the lid top left edge, one along the right edge and one centered between the sides. Remove the tape backing and sprinkle the bead mix onto the three tape strips. Use your finger to press the beads in place.

2 Wrap a length of tape around the sides of the lid, ¼" above the bottom edge. Remove the tape backing and sprinkle beads onto each side, pressing them onto the tape with your fingers.

3 Trace the heart pattern, place it on the tape roll and draw around the shape to make four hearts. Cut out the hearts. Place one centered on each side of the box. Remove the backing and sprinkle beads onto each heart, pressing them onto the tape with your fingers. Use the letter stickers to personalize the box front as shown.

17

Pink Piggy Bank

5"x4"x4¾" white ceramic piggy bank
enamel glass paints: pink, dark pink
medium point paint pens: black, aqua,
lavender, yellow
fine point paint pens: black, red
enamel gloss glaze
enamel cleaner and conditioner
flat paintbrushes: ¼", ½" wide
basic supplies (see inside the front cover)

1 Follow the manufacturer's directions to clean the ceramic surface. Paint the pig pink; let dry. Apply a second coat of pink paint; let dry. Paint the snout and inner ears dark pink; let dry.

2 Use the medium black pen to draw the nostrils and the eyes, then use the fine point black pen to draw the eyelashes. Draw four blue toenails on each hoof, ⅜" wide swirls evenly spaced on the pig and a ⅞" wide swirl for the pig's tail. Draw ¼" lavender hearts evenly spaced on the pig.

3 Draw yellow tri-dots evenly spaced on the pig. Draw single 1/16" red dots evenly spaced on the pig. Use the red pen to write your name on her left ear as shown. Apply a coat of glaze over the painted areas and let dry.

Jeweled Piggy Bank

2¾"x3" white ceramic piggy bank
dark blue enamel glass paint
fine point paint pens: black, white
3mm rhinestones: 12 pink, 23 light blue, 18 clear
enamel gloss glaze
enamel cleaner and conditioner
½" wide flat paintbrush
basic supplies (see inside the front cover)

1 Follow the manufacturer's directions to clean the ceramic surface. Paint the pig dark blue; let dry. Apply a second coat of paint; let dry. Apply a coat of glaze over the painted areas and let dry. Draw black eyes and nostrils. Use the white pen to write your name on her left ear as shown.

2 Glue a row of three pink rhinestones along the base of each ear. Glue a row of two rhinestones above the first row, then one rhinestone of the center row to form a triangle on each ear. Glue three blue rhinestones at the front of each hoof. Glue the remaining rhinestones evenly spaced on the pig.

Snack Box

5½"x4⅛"x2½" white metal lunch box
   with a 1¼" tall red plastic handle
6" of ⅝" wide white dots on yellow
   grosgrain ribbon
iron-on flower appliques: 1" wide orange,
   1" wide fuchsia, 1⅝" wide orange
fine point paint pens: black, yellow
Fat Caps alphabet template
basic supplies (see inside the front cover)

1 Fold ¼" on each end of the
ribbon, then glue it to the left
side of the box lid, wrapping the
ends to the sides. Glue the flowers
to the ribbon as shown.

2 Use the template and black
pen to trace the letters spelling
"SNACK BOX" on the lid, then write
your name above the word "SNACK". Use the
yellow pen to fill in the template letters, then draw a
loopy line border along the lid front edge. Draw black
tri-dots evenly spaced on the lid.

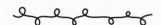

Earrings Box

2¼"x3½"x1" plastic box with inside dividers and hinged lid
   adhesive-back craft foam shapes: one 1⅞" wide red gingham
   flower, one 1" wide yellow gingham flower, two 1" green
   leaves, one ⅜" wide orange circle
fine tip paint pens: black, green, red
   basic supplies (see inside the front cover)

1 Remove the backing from the orange circle and place it
centered on the yellow flower, then place the yellow flower
centered on the red flower. Place the flower centered on the lid
top. Place the leaves below the flower as shown.

2 Draw a green line below the flower and through the
leaves as shown. Draw ⅜" wide squiggle line stripes
evenly spaced along the box sides, then color each stripe
green. Draw a column of three red dots between each
pair of stripes.

3 Draw a black dash-dot border along the outer edge of
the flowers and circle, then draw the leaf veins. Draw
a black squiggle line and dot border along the lid top outer edge, then
personalize it as shown.

19

Paw Prints Frame

3¼"x4" white ceramic frame with a 1⅝"x2¼" opening
⁷⁄₁₆" red ball & stick letter and number stickers
black dimensional paint
basic supplies (see inside the front cover)

Apply the stickers to the top and bottom of the farme as shown. Hold the paint bottle straight down and squeeze lightly to make a ¼" wide black dot, then make four ⅛" wide dots around the top to form a paw print. Repeat to form paw prints along the sides of the frame as shown and let dry. Insert your photo into the frame.

> **LeNae Says:** *Make the treats box even more personal by using paint colors that match those of your dog!*

Dog Treats Box

3½"x3½"x6⅛" clear acrylic box
3½"x4" unfinished wood dog shape
15" of ⅝" wide black/white gingham ribbon
dimensional paints: black, red, white
medium brown acrylic paint
black fine point paint pen
½" wide flat paintbrush
tracing paper, transfer paper
basic supplies (see inside the front cover)

1 Paint the front and back of the wood dog brown and let dry. Trace and transfer (see the inside back cover) the dog pattern (see inside the front cover) onto the dog shape. Use the pen to draw the lines and face features, then use the dimensional paint to fill in the nose and the spots; let dry. Draw a red line across the dog's neck for a collar; let dry. Glue the dog to the box flush with the bottom edge.

2 Glue the ribbon around the lid sides, ¼" above the bottom edge. Use the red paint to write "Treats" centered on the lid top and the dog's name on the three empty sides of the box; let dry. For the bones: Draw a ⅜" white line in a corner of the lid top, then make two dots at each end. Repeat for a bone in each corner. Follow the directions in the project above to make paw prints along the upper sides of the lid; let dry.

Baseball Cap Bank

2³/₄"x3¹/₂"1¹/₂" white ceramic
    baseball cap bank
⁷/₁₆" black letter stickers
red enamel glass paint
black fine point paint pen

enamel cleaner and
    conditioner
enamel gloss glaze
¹/₂" wide flat paintbrush
basic supplies (see inside the
    front cover)

1 Follow the manufacturer's directions to clean the
ceramic surface. Paint the cap red; let dry. Apply a
second coat of paint; let dry. Apply a coat of glaze over
the painted area and let dry.

2 Draw stitch lines around the brim and seams. Use
the letter stickers to personalize the cap.

LeNae's Suggestion: *This cap makes a
perfect gift for each member of the team.
Make one for each player and hand them
out at the end-of-season party.*

Cat Treats Tin

4"x5" white metal round tin
¹/₂" black craft foam
    self-adhesive alphabet letters
craft foam self-adhesive 2¹/₄"
    cats: 1 blue,1 purple, 1 pink,
    1 yellow, 1 orange
craft foam self-adhesive
    circles: four ³/₈" yellow, four
    ³/₈" lime green, four ³/₈" pink,
    two ¹/₄" pink, two ¹/₄" yellow,
    one ¹/₄" lime green

craft foam ¹/₂" wide
    self-adhesive flowers with
    removable centers: 5 pink,
    5 yellow, 5 lime green
tracing paper, transfer paper
basic supplies (see inside the
    front cover)

1 Trace and transfer (see inside the back cover) the cat face
to the lid center top, then use the pen to outline the face
features. Remove the backing and place the foam letters around
the lid edges to personalize the tin.

2 Remove the backing and place the foam cats evenly
spaced along the bottom edge of the tin. Place the ¹/₄"
foam circles evenly spaced between the cats. Place green,
yellow and pink foam flower clusters around the tin as shown.
Place the large circles, alternating colors, evenly spaced around
the lid sides.

3 Draw a black dot on each large foam circle, then draw a
¹/₈" line between each pair of circles. Draw swirl lines and
dots near the flower clusters as shown.

Trick or Treat Tin Pail

6¾"x7¼" round white metal pail with
   handle
acrylic paints for metal: black, orange,
   dark purple, dark green
medium point paint pens: black, red,
   brown, dark green
fine point paint pen: dark green
black dimensional paint
two 2½"x4" pieces of compressed sponge
tracing paper
paper plate
basic supplies (see inside the front cover)

1 Trace the pumpkin patterns and cut out each from the sponge. Pour a quarter size puddle of orange paint onto the paper plate. Moisten the sponges and dip them into the paint. Press the large pumpkin at the center bottom of the pail. Press the small pumpkin to the right of the large pumpkin, then press it again overlapping the large on the left side; let dry.

2 Draw a ¼" brown stem on each pumpkin top. Use the medium point pen to draw green tendrils on each pumpkin and let dry. Paint dark green leaves on the pumpkins as shown; let dry. Draw black lines down the center of each leaf and dash-dot seams on the pumpkins; let dry. Use the fine point green pen to draw a dash-line border along the pail top; let dry.

3 For the lid: Pour a quarter size puddle of black paint onto the paper plate. Rinse a sponge, dip it into the paint and press it along the lid sides; let dry. Draw a black swirl, beginning at the lid center and extending out to the outer edge. Draw straight lines dividing the lid into eight pie shapes; let dry. Draw two black spiders onto the lid as shown. Add two red dots for eyes on each spider.

4 Place the pail on its side with the front up and use the dimensional paint to write "Trick or Treat" and personalize the pail; let dry. Trace two bats onto the pail as shown. Fill in each bat with black dimensional paint; let dry. Add red dots for eyes on each bat.

Halloween Box

2¼"x2¼"x3" clear acrylic box
7/16" black letter stickers
Paper Pizazz™ Annie Lang's
   Halloween Stickers
18" of white dots on black satin
   ribbon with wire edges

18" of ⅛" wide orange
   satin ribbon
candy corn
basic supplies (see
   inside the front cover)

1 Wash the box in warm soapy water, rinse and let dry. Fill the box with candy. Place the lid on the box. Place spider stickers over the lid seal at the left front and right back. Place the devil sticker on the center back. Place the ghost sticker on the front, then place two more spiders on the front as shown. Use the letter stickers to personalize the box above the ghost.

2 Place the orange ribbon centered on the dots ribbon, wrap them around the box to the top and knot to secure. Cut an inverted "V" into each dots ribbon tail. Trim each orange tail at an angle.

Heart Boxes

clear acrylic boxes: one 2¼"x2¼"x4",
   one 2¼"x2¼"x5"
⁵⁄₁₆" red ball & stick letter stickers
red acrylic paint
glitter paints: red, clear
Deco Art Styrene™ painting blank
heart punches: ½", ¾" wide
two 1¼" wide wood knobs
½" wide flat paintbrush
basic supplies (see inside the front
   cover)

1 Squeeze the red glitter paint onto
   half of the painting blank, then
squeeze the clear onto the other half,
leaving a small space between the
two colors. Use your finger to spread
the paint evenly on the blank, then
place the blank in an undisturbed
area and let dry overnight. Peel the
paint layers off the blank.

Holiday Cookie Pail

6¾"x7¼" round white metal pail
   with handle
compressed sponges: one 4"x5",
   one 1" square
medium point paint pens: green, black
acrylic paints: brown, red
dimensional paints: white, green, red
twelve 15" strands of dark green raffia
acrylic matte spray sealer
natural excelsior (enough to fill pail)
paper plate
1" wide masking tape
4" cookie cutters: one green tree,
   one red gingerbread boy
optional: home-baked cookies
tracing paper
basic supplies (see inside
   the front cover)

1 Remove the lid and
   spray each piece with
sealer; let dry. Place masking
tape under the ridge near the pail
top, then another piece ⅜" below
the first piece. Pour a quarter size
puddle of red paint onto the paper
plate. Moisten the 1" sponge, dip
it into the paint and press it along
the exposed area between the tape
strips and let dry. Sponge the lid
top red and let dry.

2 For the tall heart box: Punch eight ¾" and four
   ½" hearts from the red layer and eight ½" hearts
from the clear layer. Place a clear heart on each
large heart, then press them onto the box front as
shown. Press a small red heart onto each corner
of the lid. Paint the knob red and let dry. Glue the
knob centered onto the lid top and let dry.

3 For the short heart box: Punch fifteen ½"
   red hearts and one ¾" clear heart. Press
three red hearts evenly spaced along the bottom
edge of each box side. Place one red heart
centered on the clear heart, then place the
heart centered on the lid front side.
Press a red heart on each side of the
clear heart. Paint the knob red and
let dry. Glue the knob centered onto
the lid top and let dry. Use the letter
stickers to personalize the box front.

2 Trace the gingerbread
   shape and cut it out. Place
it on the large sponge and cut
the shape out. Pour brown paint
onto the paper place. Moisten
the sponge, dip it into the paint

and press it onto the pail side at
a slight angle. Repeat at various
angles evenly spaced around
the pail; let dry.

3 Use the black pen to
   personalize the lid top.
Draw a green dotted scallop
border around the lid edge.
Repeat the dotted scallop
border along the pail top and
bottom edges. Write "Merry
Christmas" above the red
stripe. Spray the painted areas
with sealer and let dry.

4 Draw white squiggle lines
   on the arms and legs of
each gingerbread boy, a green
bow tie, three red dots below
the bow tie and a black mouth
and eyes. Insert the excelsior
into the pail. Hold the raffia
strands together and knot them
around the handle. Insert the
excelsior, cutters and cookies
into the tin and place the lid
on top.

Felt Hearts Round Tin

4"x5" white round metal tin
felt: dark green, medium blue, burgundy, purple
ten 3⁄8" wide ivory/tan buttons
ivory embroidery floss
sewing needle
tracing paper
basic supplies (see inside the front cover)

1 Cut a 13"x1¾" strip of green felt. Thread the needle with three strands of floss, then sew a running stitch (see inside the back cover) along each long edge. Sew nine buttons evenly spaced along the strip, beginning 2" from each end. Wrap the strip around the tin center and glue the ends at the front.

2 Trace the circle and the 3" and 1½" wide hearts and cut each out. Cut from the felt a blue circle, large purple heart and two small burgundy hearts. Sew a running stitch around the purple and circle's edges. Sew your name on a burgundy heart, then sew it centered on the purple heart as shown. Glue the purple heart centered on the circle, then glue the circle onto the tin front, centered between the buttons on the strip.

3 Cut one 2" and thirteen 3⁄8" squares of green felt. Sew a button to the remaining heart center, then sew the heart to the 2" square as shown. Sew an "X" in each corner of the square, then glue it centered onto the lid. Glue the small squares evenly spaced around the lid sides.

1½" heart

Felt Hearts Lunch Box

3" wide heart

7⁄8" heart

5½"x4⅛"x2½" white metal lunch box with a 1¼" tall red plastic handle
felt: dark green, medium blue, burgundy, purple
one ¼" wide ivory/tan button
ivory embroidery floss
sewing needle
tracing paper
basic supplies (see inside the front cover)

1 Trace the 1⅝" and 7⁄8" hearts and cut them out. Cut from the felt one large purple heart; one small green and two small burgundy hearts. Cut a blue 4⅛"x3⅛" and a green 4½"x3½" felt rectangle.

2 Thread the needle with three strands of floss. Sew the button to the green heart, then sew the green heart to the purple heart as shown. Sew the purple heart centered on the blue rectangle, then sew a burgundy heart on each side. Sew your name in the upper right corner of

1⅝" heart

the blue rectangle. Sew it centered on the green rectangle, then glue it to the box front. Cut eleven ¾"x1⅛" green felt rectangles. Glue them evenly spaced around the sides of the box.